365 DAILY AFFIRMATIONS
For Time Management

D1304537

Praise for

365 Daily Affirmations for Time Management

"Jan Yager has a knack for getting to the heart of time management fundamentals, from simply being in control of your time, to savoring every moment. This book will help you every day to be all that you can be for yourself, your family, and for the rest of us."

—Martin Zwilling, author of
Do You Have What It Takes To Be An Entrepreneur?

"Yager's affirmations are as practical as they can be, and quietly powerful as well."

—Victoria Moran, author of *Creating a Charmed Life*

"Read this book for inspiration, motivation, and insights into how to improve the way you handle your time work or leisure time. I love this book! It's a gem!"

—Julie Jansen, author,
I Don't Know What I Want, But I Know It's Not This

"In today's fast paced world that is often chaotic, demanding and stressful, Dr Jan Yager's *365 Daily Affirmations for Time Management* is a terrific little book that will help you to find or regain balance in your life."

—Donna Hanson, computer productivity trainer, Director, Prime Solutions (Victoria, Australia)

"Dr. Jan Yager's 365 affirmations and quotes, and especially the lessons from her father, are really helpful. I am already using these insights in my life."

—Kanak Kr Jain, CFP, Suskan Consultans Pvt Ltd, Kolkata, India

" Time is the most precious commodity on the market today. My passion is helping people create a 'productive environment' so they can accomplish their work and enjoy their lives. Keeping Jan Yager's latest book in a prominent place in your home or office is a great step to making that happen in your life!"

—Barbara Hemphill, author, *Taming the Paper Tiger* series

365 DAILY AFFIRMATIONS

For Time Management

Jan Yager, Ph.D.

HANNACROIX CREEK BOOKS, INC.
Stamford, Connecticut

This book is dedicated, with love,
to my husband Fred, our sons, Scott and Jeff, Nicole,
and our grandson Bradley

Cover design by Scribe Freelance | www.scribefreelance.com

Published by:
Hannacroix Creek Books, Inc.
1127 High Ridge Road, #110
Stamford, Connecticut 06905 USA
http://www.hannacroixcreekbooks.com
E-mail: hannacroix@aol.com
Follow us on twitter: www.twitter.com/hannacroixcreek

ISBN: 978-1-889262-95-6 (trade paperback)

ISBN: 978-1-889262-56-7 (hardcover)

Library of Congress Cataloging-in-Publication Data

Yager, Jan, 1948-
  365 daily affirmations for time management / Jan Yager.
    p. cm.
  ISBN 978-1-889262-56-7 (hardcover) -- ISBN 978-1-889262-95-6
(trade pbk.)
1. Time management--Miscellanea. I. Title. II. Title: Three hundred
sixty-five daily affirmations for time management.
  HD69.T54Y3338 2011
  650.1'1--dc22
                                2010024025

Contents

Introduction

The world can seem to spin out of control when the demands on us from work and from others keep expanding, while the available number of hours in the day is still just twenty-four. This little book will help you to regain control and to find peace from within as you master the most valuable commodity that any of us have at our fingertips: our time.

Time is a concept that has been pondered and studied over the centuries by philosophers, poets, essayists, anthropologists, sociologists, psychologists, authors, efficiency experts, and intellectuals.

Affirmations about time are a wonderful way to celebrate whatever time each of us has on this earth. They also provide a positive framework for the self-concepts that can help you to be more efficient, productive, and effective.

The first affirmation in this book is definitely my favorite because in these frenzied times when there does not seem to be enough hours in the day or days in the week, it says it all: *"I am in control of how I manage my time."*

I find that an affirming thought: that I *am* in control of how I manage my time.

How about you? Do you feel in control of how you manage your time? Your time at work? Your leisure time? Your time at school? If you do not feel in control, how can you remedy that? You will find several hundred affirmations in this book to help you to gain or regain control of your time. You *can* accomplish your priority tasks for this minute, this hour, and this day. You *can* decide what you need to do, what you would like to do, or what you absolutely must do, and then get it done.

You will also find sprinkled throughout this book of time management affirmations some of my favorite famous quotes about time and time management principles including getting organized such as this one from Benjamin Franklin, who wrote, "A place for everything, everything in its place" or from essayist Henry David Thoreau, who wrote, "Our life is frittered away by detail... Simplify, simplify."

•

Frederick Winslow Taylor's book, *The Principles of Scientific Management*, published in 1911, exposes his views on how to increase the productivity of workers. Some of his findings, which today may seem like common sense, back then were considered revolutionary:

- Giving incentives to employees to become more productive could lead to greater achievements

- It would increase productivity if it became known what the optimal number of rest periods during the workday were and to allow for that pacing.

- Offering training to workers to help them to do their jobs rather than depending on self-training would lead to more efficiency.

Today, time management is a topic that is very much in vogue. There are time management coaches, speakers, trainers, authors, and researchers. We can learn a lot from all of these time management gurus, especially the researchers. Here is just one example, as I point out in my book *Work Less, Do More* (Sterling, 2008): a 1999 Cornell University study found that those who had occasional onscreen reminders that they should take a break made 13% fewer errors than those who did not.

I have been studying time management since my early thirties, when I was single and completely absorbed in my career. As my life has changed—I married in my mid-thirties and my husband and I became parents to two sons as I took some time off from work for fulltime parenting followed by part-time self-employment and years of college level part-time teaching as I juggled working, being a wife, mother, and also trying to make some time for friends and extended family—I noticed a change not only in my own pushes and pulls but in the society around me, as it relates to time and time management. Since I travel a lot for business, I also noticed that countries that were completely disinterested in the concept of time management in the 1980s or even the 1990s, were eager to learn about it and spread those principles to their countrymen and women after the new millennium.

Suddenly the terms that I had learned from the seminars I took, and the readings and original research I had conducted, were becoming part of the everyday vocabulary of a very diverse group of people. Terms like "work-life balance," "prioritizing," "goal setting," and "procrastination" were key concepts for achieving more but in less time and with less stress for everyone from self-employed entrepreneurs and small business owners to those who worked for the government and in major corporations employing tens of thousands of workers.

Speed versus Making the Right Choices

When I was offering workshops, and reviewing my own career and life, I had an epiphany that I want to share with you now—and I know that others have said this as well but for me it was a very powerful realization—*it is not just how fast you do anything but making sure you are doing the right thing in the first place.*

But here is the Catch-22. How do you *know* if you're doing the "right" thing? Usually by the results. But what if the results are days, weeks, years, or even decades into the future?

Yet I have observed that if you get good at this skill called time management, and even better at trusting your gut and the feelings within yourself if something or someone is working out, you will start to get better at stopping yourself before you have invested weeks, months, years or even decades in activities or relationships that just were not quite right for you.

The benefit of the tools of time management is that those tools—like organizing your papers and your things so you are in control of your possessions, or being on time so you do not make others angry or upset—are just superficial tools to the far more important mental work that each and every one of us has to do so that we are truly making the most of the precious time we have on earth.

Perhaps one of the most dramatic recent examples of someone who knew that his time was short and who taught the world the lesson of making the most of each moment was computer science professor Randy Pausch. Battling pancreatic cancer, 47-year old Dr. Pausch delivered his last lecture, "Really Achieving Your Childhood Dreams," to 400 people at Carnegie Mellon University. That lecture, which was recorded and put on youtube.com, became an international phenomenon. *Wall Street Journal* reporter Jeffrey Zaslow, who was at the lecture, co-authored a book with Randy Pausch, *The Last Lecture,* which became an international bestseller, with translations into 40 languages. A year and a half after that lecture, Dr. Pausch, the happily married father of three young children, died from cancer. But he had lived his life to the fullest, and he left a legacy of that message in his video presentation and in his book and of course through his relationships with his children, wife, extended family, friends, and colleagues.

Randy Pausch is just one of the countless examples of those who have died before their time. Since none of us knows how much time one has on this earth, it is worthwhile to ask yourself this question: *Am I making the most of my time?* It is not just accomplishing more at work that we all seek. As it is often said, no one in the face of death says that he or she wishes to have spent more time at work or at the office! What we all seek is a *balanced* life filled with people, memorable experiences, and work that is rewarding and lucrative enough to enable us to keep a roof over our heads, food in our belly, clothes on our back, and as much or as little extra materialism as each person needs or craves.

This time management affirmations book is based on the principle behind affirmations in general, namely that by reinforcing positive ideas and concepts, your reality will shift as you gradually substitute positive thoughts and actions for negative ones. This book, however, is *not* meant to be a substitute for seeking out professional help if that is what you need for your time management challenges, whether you need to be in treatment with a psychiatrist, psychologist, social worker, or another type of mental health professional.

This book will hopefully help you to get more out of each day since all of us are being asked to do more by others as we also put greater demands on ourselves.

Research has found that being positive is a technique that can help us to achieve more as well as to reduce stress and frustration. So whether or not your boss appreciates you, and whether or not you feel you're as productive as you can be, reading all these affirmations straight through, or just reading one each day, every day, is a technique that could help you to simultaneously achieve inner peace and greater productivity.

After the 365 daily time management affirmations, there is a place in this book for you to write down your own affirmations if you choose to do so. Then you will find in Part 2 activities to help you to improve your time management at work and in your personal life. I hope you find these activities motivating and fun!

I share at the end of the book, in Part 3, the three time management lessons that my father taught me. I hope this essay will inspire you to consider the time management lessons that your father or mother and even your siblings or your first boss taught you and how that has shaped your own time attitudes or behavior.

There are plenty of additional books on time management; you will find some of the top books listed in the Bibliography. You will also find time management resources in the Resources.

I welcome hearing from you about your favorite affirmations in this collection as well as what affirmations you write for yourself. Although a personal reply cannot be guaranteed, I want to thank you in advance for writing to me. Here is my contact information: Dr. Jan Yager, P.O. Box 8038, Stamford, Connecticut 06905-8038 USA, jyager@aol.com. You can also follow me on twitter: www.twitter.com/drjanyager.

For free excerpts from some of my books, reprints of published articles, and my original blog, please visit my website: www.drjanyager.com

I appreciate you, my reader, and thank you for taking the time to read 365 *Daily Affirmations for Time Management.*

Happy reading!

Dr. Jan Yager

PART I

365 DAILY AFFIRMATIONS
For Time Management

1

I am in control of how I manage my time.

■ ■ ■

2

Today I am figuring out what I need
to do to succeed, and I am focusing
my energies on those actions.

■ ■ ■

3

I make each minute count.

■ ■ ■

4

I am aware that any chaos I feel within will be
reflected in how I manage my time so I am taking
care to minimize or eliminate any internal chaos.

■ ■ ■

5

I have work and life balance.

■ ■ ■

6

I have goals.

■ ■ ■

7
I am calm.

■ ■ ■

8
I am organized.

■ ■ ■

9
I know that the only person I can control is myself
so I am focusing on controlling myself.

■ ■ ■

10
I am grateful for the people
I love and that love me.

■ ■ ■

11
I am inspired to make the
most of each and every day.

■ ■ ■

12
I am living in the now.

■ ■ ■

13
I am doing my best.

■ ■ ■

14
I am prioritizing all that I have to do
with the most important thing first.

■ ■ ■

15
I am embracing the household chores and finding
joy in creating order in how things are organized.

■ ■ ■

16
I am delegating to others if it is in my best interest
to do that; or doing everything myself
if that is the better option.

■ ■ ■

17
I am observing those who are excellent time
managers so I can learn from their examples.

■ ■ ■

18
I am pacing myself.

■ ■ ■

19
I am taking time off so I am
replenished and well-rested.

■ ■ ■

20
I aim for an excellence that is achievable.

■ ■ ■

21
I make the time for my friends
and extended family.

■ ■ ■

22
I keep active and inactive things separated
so that I can find my day-to-day
and priority materials quickly.

■ ■ ■

23
I take the time to put everything back in its place.
■ ■ ■

24
I group and do similar tasks together.
■ ■ ■

25
I stop and smell the flowers.
■ ■ ■

26
I deal with coworkers, clients, and employees
in a formal but pleasant manner.
■ ■ ■

27
I make clear decisions and have
sharp decision-making skills.
■ ■ ■

28
I respond to business correspondence promptly.
■ ■ ■

29
I return business phone calls
within twenty-four hours.

■ ■ ■

30
I keep up with the latest technology.

■ ■ ■

31
I am aware that emotional crises will
impact on how someone handles times,
so I cut myself and others some slack.

■ ■ ■

32
I am persistent.

■ ■ ■

33
I know the only person I can control is myself,
so I begin by changing anything about
myself that I so choose.

■ ■ ■

34
I keep myself engaged and energized every day
with stimulating and motivational activities.
■ ■ ■

35
I recognize jealousy in myself and turn it
into something effective and productive.
■ ■ ■

36
I am on top of my files by having
a regular sift-and-purge schedule.
■ ■ ■

37
I am aware of how long I am on the phone.
■ ■ ■

38
I read.
■ ■ ■

39
I talk with and listen to friends.
■ ■ ■

40
I value my family.

■ ■ ■

41
Being organized is a trait I am learning.

■ ■ ■

42
I am a self-actualizing person because
that means that I value my time and
make wise choices about how I spend it.

■ ■ ■

43
I am benefiting from the words of psychologist
Alan Wheelis who, in his book *How People Change*,
writes: "Personality change follows change in
behavior. Since we are what we do, if we want
to change what we are we must begin by
changing what we do, [and] must
undertake a new mode of action."

■ ■ ■

44
I have expectations that are
realistic and attainable.
■ ■ ■

45
I am honest.
■ ■ ■

46
I am trustworthy.
■ ■ ■

47
I have a mental or written "to do" list
that guides what I need to accomplish today.
■ ■ ■

48
I know that it is more important to do the right
things than to be busy so I am taking the time to
figure out what I should be doing with my time.
■ ■ ■

49
I meditate to reduce tension and stress.
■ ■ ■

50
I focus.
■ ■ ■

51
I make the most of my commuting time.
■ ■ ■

52
I accept feedback with gratitude
and use what is valuable to me.
■ ■ ■

53
Today I remind myself of the
long-term goals I have set for myself.
■ ■ ■

54
Today I review my short-term goals and
the steps I have devised to achieve those goals.
■ ■ ■

55
I am comfortable asking for help.

■ ■ ■

56
I exercise regularly.

■ ■ ■

57
I save time by communicating clearly,
whether verbally or nonverbally.

■ ■ ■

58
I appreciate what I have achieved in the past
as I stay focused on the present
while still being aware of the future.

■ ■ ■

59
I am patient with those who need to learn how
to work more effectively as I help them to
understand techniques and tools for efficiency.

■ ■ ■

60
I learn from the past as I try
hard to be the best I can be.

■ ■ ■

61
Today I remind myself that my time management
effectiveness is within my own hands.

■ ■ ■

62
Today I embrace new ways of
more effectively managing my time.

■ ■ ■

63
Today I am a go-getter.

■ ■ ■

64
I am making the most of every single
second, minute, and hour in this one day.

■ ■ ■

65
Today I am courageous.
■ ■ ■

66
Today I am empathetic toward the plight of others.
■ ■ ■

67
Today I find the time to volunteer to help others who are less fortunate.
■ ■ ■

68
I listen to my children without judgment.
■ ■ ■

69
I appreciate my spouse and listen as if we have just met and are getting to know each other for the first time.
■ ■ ■

70

I am working on as many tasks
as I can manage successfully.

■ ■ ■

71

I feel the power of more
effective time management.

■ ■ ■

72

I am leaving my previous
unproductive habits behind.

■ ■ ■

73

I am planning for efficiency breaks because
pacing myself reduces my stress and makes
me more efficient and effective.

■ ■ ■

74

I am learning to say and hear "no"
without taking it personally.

■ ■ ■

75
I am concentrating.

■ ■ ■

76
Today I am pleasing myself.

■ ■ ■

77
I am recognizing any signs of burnout in myself and redirecting my time so I can become replenished.

■ ■ ■

78
I ask my children to do chores because independence builds their sense of empowerment.

■ ■ ■

79
Today I put as much effort into how I spend my personal time as to how I spend my work time.

■ ■ ■

80
Today I appreciate the differences in people and that some are more productive than others.

■ ■ ■

81
I reward myself for staying focused.

■ ■ ■

82
I value my weekend time.

■ ■ ■

83
I leave some free time every day in case there is a new urgent priority I have to deal with.

■ ■ ■

84
I am flexible.

■ ■ ■

85
Today I plan.

■ ■ ■

86
I see filing and paperwork as part of my job and I make the time to deal with it on a regular basis.

■ ■ ■

87
I am thankful for every moment.

■ ■ ■

88
I am learning when I need to focus my attention on one person exclusively, and when I need to expand my horizons and deal with others as well.

■ ■ ■

89
Today I am re-evaluating the technology I use to see if I have to change or upgrade those tools.

■ ■ ■

90
I have a database of contacts so I have easy access to the contact information for those I need to communicate with regularly.

■ ■ ■

91
I create realistic and attainable
deadlines to guide my activities.

■ ■ ■

92
I backup my work on the computer in multiple
ways so I do not fear losing my efforts if there is a
hard drive crash or any other kind of malfunction.

■ ■ ■

93
I emulate the strategies of those who
handle their time well as I develop my
own unique time management systems.

■ ■ ■

94
If I feel envy, I understand why I feel that way
as I put the emphasis on what I do have.

■ ■ ■

95
I carefully review everything I write.

■ ■ ■

96
Today I can remember.

■ ■ ■

97
I have enough time.

■ ■ ■

98
I am enjoying every relationship, every moment,
and every task to the fullest.

■ ■ ■

99
I am learning from all the experiences
and relationships I have had before this day.

■ ■ ■

100
I am decisive about what
to keep and what to toss out.

■ ■ ■

101
I am grateful for the time I have with my children.

■ ■ ■

102

I cherish the time I spend
with my romantic partner.

■ ■ ■

103

I pay attention to my dreams.

■ ■ ■

104

Today is the first day of forever.

■ ■ ■

105

Today I am putting all the positive energy and
thoughts I can muster to make this day as
productive and memorable as it can be.

■ ■ ■

106

I am open to new ideas and experiences.

■ ■ ■

107

I welcome the efficiency that technology
can bring to my work but I also make sure
technology suits me and my individual needs.

■ ■ ■

108

I am careful to back up my work on the computer
because that is a way of reaffirming
the value of myself and what I do.

■ ■ ■

109

I am following my passions.

■ ■ ■

110

I see procrastination as information by asking
myself the key question, "*Why* am I putting off
doing what I know I should be doing now?"

■ ■ ■

111

I respect the time limitations of others and I am
accepting of their time challenges if someone
cannot find the time to meet with me.

■ ■ ■

112
How I spend my time is a choice and
I make that choice with care and thought.

■ ■ ■

113
I set aside time to deal with the daily
concerns that require my attention.

■ ■ ■

114
I study the time habits of those who are
successful and efficient but I know that
the methods I have developed for myself
are the ones that matter the most.

■ ■ ■

115
I take the time to study time
management if it is useful for me.

■ ■ ■

116
I am attuned to my energy highs and lows
as I use that valuable self-awareness
to plan my day more effectively.

■ ■ ■

117
I am patient with those who are
less energetic or organized than me.

■ ■ ■

118
I only delegate if it is in my best interest,
not as a sign of power or status.

■ ■ ■

119
I spend time with my loved ones.

■ ■ ■

120
I strive for excellence,
not an unrealistic perfectionism.

■ ■ ■

121
I use my waiting time—in airports, offices,
train stations, restaurants—wisely.

■ ■ ■

122
I make time each day to reflect on my daily
activities as well as my short and long-term goals.

■ ■ ■

123
"How much time he gains who does not look to
see what his neighbor says or does or thinks."
— Marcus Aurelius

■ ■ ■

124
I get back to those who contact me as soon
as possible but I am understanding if others
are not as efficient or prompt in return.

■ ■ ■

125
I practice polite but firm ways to get off the phone
if a conversation is going on longer than the time I
have for it or if I need to go somewhere else.

■ ■ ■

126
I am careful about multitasking and only
do more than one task simultaneously if it
does not put me or anyone else in jeopardy.
■ ■ ■

127
I am an effective time manager.
■ ■ ■

128
"Remember that time is money."
— Benjamin Franklin
■ ■ ■

129
I deal with incoming correspondence
or e-mails in a timely manner.
■ ■ ■

130
I have a filing system that works for me.
■ ■ ■

131
I am aware of the time demands on me
and I am in control of those demands.

■ ■ ■

132
I design or redesign my work space
so I have optimum working conditions.

■ ■ ■

133
"More men are killed by overwork than
the importance of the world justifies."
—Rudyard Kipling

■ ■ ■

134
I take the time to sort and sift through
my papers, magazines, and other items.

■ ■ ■

135
I am in control of my clutter.

■ ■ ■

136
I make vacation time a priority.

■ ■ ■

137
I make weekend time away
from work a main concern.

■ ■ ■

138
I research so I benefit from
the knowledge of others.

■ ■ ■

139
I make the time to keep up with new trends.

■ ■ ■

140
"Lost time is never found again."
—Benjamin Franklin

■ ■ ■

141
I allow myself to relax
without feeling guilty about it.

■ ■ ■

142
I make the time for appropriate physical intimacy.

■ ■ ■

143
I avoid wasting the time of others.

■ ■ ■

144
I put my family first.

■ ■ ■

145
I consider what expert Robert Rutherford refers to
as LOPOs (low-payoff activities) and HIPOs
(high-payoff activities), putting more of
my time in the HIPOs than the LOPOs.

■ ■ ■

146
I reduce stress by planning
(not over planning) and exercising.

■ ■ ■

147
I use Pareto's law – that 20% of my efforts will yield
80% of my results – to help plan my day, figuring
out what the 20% and what the 80% will be.

■ ■ ■

148
I am comfortable saying "no."

■ ■ ■

149
I am okay with hearing "no."

■ ■ ■

150
I see comments about my performance or
about me as feedback rather than as criticism.

■ ■ ■

151
"It has been my observation that most people get ahead during the time that others waste."

— Henry Ford
■ ■ ■

152
I only watch as much television as I feel is beneficial to me.
■ ■ ■

153
Today I am identifying one habit that is interfering with more effective time management and working on changing that habit.
■ ■ ■

154
"If we all did the things we are capable of doing, we would literally astound ourselves."

— Thomas A. Edison
■ ■ ■

155
Today I am valuing — not devaluing or
overvaluing— myself and my activities.
■ ■ ■

156
I am grateful for everything and
everyone in my life.
■ ■ ■

157
I respect that others may manage
their time or even consider time
in a different way than my views.
■ ■ ■

158
I am rewarding myself for going forward
on a task that I would rather put off doing.
■ ■ ■

159
"A man is what he thinks about all day long."
— Ralph Waldo Emerson
■ ■ ■

160
I know that others are trying their best.
■ ■ ■

161
I am learning every day from every
experience and relationship in my life.
■ ■ ■

162
"Perseverance is a great element of success.
If you only knock long enough and loud enough
at the gate, you are sure to wake up somebody."
— Henry Wadsworth Longfellow
■ ■ ■

163
"A long life may not be good enough,
but a good life is long enough."
— Benjamin Franklin
■ ■ ■

164
I am my thoughts.
■ ■ ■

165
"Action may not always bring happiness;
but there is no happiness without action."
— Benjamin Disraeli
■ ■ ■

166
Today I am making every second, every minute,
every hour, and every moment count.
■ ■ ■

167
I am putting all my energy, talent,
and commitment into everything
I do and every relationship I have.
■ ■ ■

168
I am concentrating 100% on a person or task.
■ ■ ■

169
I am focusing on what I need to do, what
I want to do, and what makes me flourish.
■ ■ ■

170

"All my possessions for a moment of time."
— last words of Queen Elizabeth I (1533-1603)

■ ■ ■

171

I approach everything and
everyone with enthusiasm.

■ ■ ■

172

I reassess my goals periodically to make sure
the goals of yesterday still match the
goals and dreams of today and tomorrow.

■ ■ ■

173

I am aware of the passage of time and that makes
me appreciate even more each and every day.

■ ■ ■

174

"How we spend our days is, of course,
how we spend our lives."
— Annie Dillard

■ ■ ■

175
I am more focused on my "doing"
list than on a "to do" list.

■ ■ ■

176
There is no one organizational system and I have
a system for organization that works for me.

■ ■ ■

177
It feels good to recycle and to
care about the environment.

■ ■ ■

178
It is harder to write short than to
write long so I do what is harder.

■ ■ ■

179
I am keeping things simple.

■ ■ ■

180
I accept that change is inevitable.

■ ■ ■

181
I am taking the time to go through my files
so I have lean and up-to-date files.

■ ■ ■

182
I build efficiency breaks into
my day to control stress.

■ ■ ■

183
I am aware of the WOOs — Windows of
Opportunity — in my life and
I am making the most of each WOO.

■ ■ ■

184
I pace myself.

■ ■ ■

185
I am working because I value work.
■ ■ ■

186
I celebrate time.
■ ■ ■

187
"Time and tide wait for no man."
— Mark Twain
■ ■ ■

188
Today is glorious.
■ ■ ■

189
Today is exciting to behold.
■ ■ ■

190
I am making the most of each
and every stage in my life.
■ ■ ■

191
"No time like the present."
— Mrs. Manley (from the novel *The Lost Lover*, 1696)

■ ■ ■

192
Life begins and ends in an instant; it is
what happens in-between that is filled
with wonder, surprises, and amazement.

■ ■ ■

193
Every day when I awaken I do not know
what magical experiences are awaiting me.

■ ■ ■

194
"A place for everything, everything in its place."
— Benjamin Franklin

■ ■ ■

195
Reading and staying current
is a valuable use of my time.

■ ■ ■

196
Getting out into the world and experiencing
different places, cultures, and people
is a wonderful way to spend my time.

■ ■ ■

197
Others may help me do what I have to do
faster but I am the only one who can figure
out what I should be doing in the first place.

■ ■ ■

198
"Our life is frittered away by detail...
Simplify, simplify."
— Henry David Thoreau

■ ■ ■

199
I use selective attention so that whenever
I am dealing with someone or something,
I am totally focused on that one thing or person.

■ ■ ■

200

"To everything there is a season, and a time and purpose under heaven, A time to be born, and a time to die, A time to plant, and a time to pluck up that which is planted..."
— (Ecclesiastes 3)

■ ■ ■

201

I am productive.

■ ■ ■

202

I have a clock to tell me the time but I am not a slave to it.

■ ■ ■

203

I avoid trying to do too much at once because in trying to do too much I will end up doing less than if I try to do just what I am capable of doing especially focusing on my priorities.

■ ■ ■

204
I know my limitations but I also know
my strengths and unique capabilities.

■ ■ ■

205
I am only in competition with my best self.

■ ■ ■

206
I have "me time" everyday.

■ ■ ■

207
I remind myself of what I need to do
today and I make that today's priority.

■ ■ ■

208
I am strong enough to handle
everything that I have on my plate.

■ ■ ■

209
I may look to others for help in various
ways but I rely only on myself.

■ ■ ■

210
I am exercising my brain everyday
so I am at my peak performance.

■ ■ ■

211
I appreciate the time I spend sleeping as
a time to replenish and revive myself.

■ ■ ■

212
I know what is expected of me so
I can fulfill those expectations or even
exceed those targets if I choose to.

■ ■ ■

213
I consider filing and keeping my desk organized
as part of my job rather than as tasks
I will get around to when I find the time.

■ ■ ■

214
I believe in myself.
■ ■ ■

215
I value myself and therefore I value my time.
■ ■ ■

216
I know how I work best and
that is key to my effectiveness.
■ ■ ■

217
I take the time to observe what is going on
in the world as I watch a sunset or a
sunrise, smell the flowers, and listen to
the sounds of nature or to people's voices.
■ ■ ■

218
"Half our life is spent trying to find
something to do with the time
we have rushed through life trying to save."
— Comedian Will Rogers
■ ■ ■

219

Although no emotions are a waste of time, I am putting the time that could be spent on jealousy, bitterness, rage, and resentment into the more productive emotions of love, forgiveness, self-acceptance, gratitude, and understanding.

■ ■ ■

220

Every day I remind myself of
at least one reason to be grateful.

■ ■ ■

221

I am valuing my time whatever
my age or stage in life.

■ ■ ■

222

Waiting is an opportunity to appreciate time and to consider thoughts and feelings that I may not have time to relish when I am rushing around.

■ ■ ■

223

I have a full life.

■ ■ ■

224
Today my life is balanced.

■ ■ ■

225
I am taking the time to choose carefully
the words that I say because I know
that words can heal and words can wound.

■ ■ ■

226
I remember the wisdom in the saying
"better late than never."

■ ■ ■

227
I am strong and clear-headed.

■ ■ ■

228
I am facing up to my fears as I go
forward on those tasks that I want to do.

■ ■ ■

229
I am accepting my strengths and my weaknesses.

■ ■ ■

230
I embrace technology as a time saver.

■ ■ ■

231
I am focusing on my productivity.

■ ■ ■

232
"A fool and his time are soon parted."
— Anonymous

■ ■ ■

233
I am making time for all the
people and activities that I enjoy.

■ ■ ■

234
I separate what matters from frivolous concerns.

■ ■ ■

235
I am open to fresh approaches and new relationships.
■ ■ ■

236
I care about those who are less fortunate.
■ ■ ■

237
I am prompt.
■ ■ ■

238
Today I will make each moment a memorable one so I go to sleep tonight feeling a sense of accomplishment about how I have spent this day.
■ ■ ■

239
Today I am considering every aspect of my office and how I go about my work and if I need to make changes I am transforming my office space accordingly.
■ ■ ■

240
I use email to be in contact but not to
completely replace communicating
over the phone or in person.

■ ■ ■

241
I understand the time constraints
and challenges of others.

■ ■ ■

242
Today I am taking the time to enjoy
each meal that I eat and to appreciate
that I have clean water to drink.

■ ■ ■

243
I am living in the present with an
eye to the future and a nod to the
memories and the lessons from the past.

■ ■ ■

244
Whether by meditating or by putting aside some
quiet uninterrupted time each day, I am pacing
myself each day so I do not burn out or stress out.
■ ■ ■

245
I have positive thoughts about
time and my productivity.
■ ■ ■

246
I am handling any pressure from
work or from my personal life.
■ ■ ■

247
I break down all the tasks and chores
I have to do each day into smaller steps
and activities that I am accomplishing.
■ ■ ■

248
I take care of my body.
■ ■ ■

249
I take care of my psyche.

■ ■ ■

250
I take the time to research and to document my findings so I can achieve my goals as efficiently as possible.

■ ■ ■

251
I am competent and successful.

■ ■ ■

252
Today I appreciate that I have this day.

■ ■ ■

253
I am adaptable.

■ ■ ■

254

I see interruptions as a necessary part
of work and life and I can handle
any disruptions that come my way.

■ ■ ■

255

I memorize a fact, a name, a number,
every day as a way of working on my memory.

■ ■ ■

256

I periodically have an Organization Day
that enables me to focus on
any clutter in my home or office.

■ ■ ■

257

I am focusing on the #1 priority project for today.

■ ■ ■

258

I am creative.

■ ■ ■

259
I notice when I lose track of time and I relish when that happens and gain understanding about myself from those experiences of timelessness.

■ ■ ■

260
I matter.

■ ■ ■

261
I concentrate by focusing from within and creating as distraction-free environment as I can manage.

■ ■ ■

262
I plan.

■ ■ ■

263
I am spontaneous.

■ ■ ■

264
I have free time each day in case
something unexpected comes up.
■ ■ ■

265
I am tackling the hardest task first.
■ ■ ■

266
I have a positive attitude.
■ ■ ■

267
I respect the ideas of others.
■ ■ ■

268
I give credit to others for their ideas.
■ ■ ■

269
I share my work and I also
protect my original work.
■ ■ ■

270
I value myself.

■ ■ ■

271
I finish what I start.

■ ■ ■

272
Today I am staying focused on what I need
to do by effectively managing any interruptions
or distractions that could throw me off my course.

■ ■ ■

273
I treat each and every person in my life as
the valued individual that he or she is.

■ ■ ■

274
I am unique.

■ ■ ■

275
Today I delegate to technology or to another
person as I continue to monitor the results.

■ ■ ■

276
"Time is the most valuable
thing a man can spend."
—Theophrastus (c. 371-c. 278 B.C.)

■ ■ ■

277
Today I wake up extra early to catch the
sunrise and to bask in the glory of nature.

■ ■ ■

278
Today I make the time to exercise even if it
is only ten or twenty minutes out of my day.

■ ■ ■

279
Today I read my "to do" list from yesterday
and see what is still "to do"
and to work on those concerns until
I can cross off those tasks and say "done!"

■ ■ ■

280
Today I respect the varied approaches to time in diverse cultures around the world.

■ ■ ■

281
I am aware that inaction is an action.

■ ■ ■

282
I value the time I spend with my friends.

■ ■ ■

283
I am having dinner with my family.

■ ■ ■

284
I am making the time for lunch no matter how busy I am at work.

■ ■ ■

285
My desk and workspace are clutter-free and organized.

■ ■ ■

286

Today I am reinforcing positive
ways of dealing with my time.

■ ■ ■

287

I deserve effective and efficient
time management skills.

■ ■ ■

288

I am deserving of the achievement of my goals.

■ ■ ■

289

Today I will have wealth come to me
and I will value the wealth I already have.

■ ■ ■

290

I handle my time well.

■ ■ ■

291
I am always searching for new and innovative
time management ideas that will empower me.

■ ■ ■

292
I am aware of how I spend my time each day.

■ ■ ■

293
I take time management workshops
online or in person to improve my skills.

■ ■ ■

294
I take a break when I need one.

■ ■ ■

295
My lifestyle is healthy because I consider
what I am eating, I exercise regularly,
and I get the necessary sleep that I need.

■ ■ ■

296
I keep track of my thoughts and my dreams
because they are the windows to my deepest
visions.

■ ■ ■

297
I check my e-mail only as often as is productive
and necessary for my job or personal life.

■ ■ ■

298
I am reviewing my goals and project tasks
on a regular basis, adjusting deadlines
or other commitments as needed.

■ ■ ■

299
Today I am accomplishing
everything that I want to do.

■ ■ ■

300
I am performing at my highest level.

■ ■ ■

301
I am achieving my goals.

■ ■ ■

302
I am accomplishing my dreams.

■ ■ ■

303
I listen to my friends and family
whenever they share over the phone,
through e-mails, letters, or in person.

■ ■ ■

304
I am taking the time to understand what
non-verbal communication means.

■ ■ ■

305
I recognize boredom as a sign that it may be
time for me to be doing something else.

■ ■ ■

306
I take the time to listen to music.
■ ■ ■

307
I am exploring fresh ideas.
■ ■ ■

308
"O! call back yesterday, bid time return."
—William Shakespeare
■ ■ ■

309
I am replacing negative thoughts about being
busy or overwhelmed with positive affirmations
that I am handling everything that I need to do.
■ ■ ■

310
I handle my time management challenges
through affirmations, but if I need to seek out
a trained mental health professional or time
management expert, I am open to that step.
■ ■ ■

311
I remind myself that holidays are about
the people and about the shared experiences.

■ ■ ■

312
I celebrate each accomplishment.

■ ■ ■

313
I am an adaptable manager.

■ ■ ■

314
I learn from results that are less than optimum,
applauding myself for the courage
to try new and different things.

■ ■ ■

315
Time management equals self-management.

■ ■ ■

316
I am creating the optimal
work environment for me.

■ ■ ■

317
I sit on an ergonomic chair
that enhances my productivity.

■ ■ ■

318
I take notes when it will aid
my retention of information.

■ ■ ■

319
I call meetings when necessary.

■ ■ ■

320
I pay attention when I attend a meeting.

■ ■ ■

321
I am on time for meetings.

■ ■ ■

322
I brainstorm to get the creative juices flowing.

■ ■ ■

323
I am honest and tactful.

■ ■ ■

324
I am virtuous.

■ ■ ■

325
I look outside my own discipline for ideas from other jobs or vocations that I can learn from and adapt to my needs. For example, if I am writer, I might look to business leaders. If I am a chef, I might look for inspiration to the auto industry.

■ ■ ■

326
I know if I am more efficient working alone or
working in a team, and I respect and appreciate
how I make optimum use of my team
and replicate those conditions for myself,
still being as flexible as I can be.
■ ■ ■

327
I read journals, books, magazines, newspapers,
and online publications so I am
as enlightened as possible.
■ ■ ■

328
I am confident in my decisions.
■ ■ ■

329
I believe in the products or services that I sell.
■ ■ ■

330
I am innovative.
■ ■ ■

331
I am comfortable offering and receiving feedback.

■ ■ ■

332
I am caring and responsive.

■ ■ ■

333
I am energetic.

■ ■ ■

334
I put frequently used items nearby.

■ ■ ■

335
I go through my closets periodically,
reorganizing and pruning my wardrobe.

■ ■ ■

336
I need to do OPPs (Other People's Projects)
as well as MPs (My Projects),
and I find the time to do both.

■ ■ ■

337
I am handling the multiple demands
on me from work or school.

■ ■ ■

338
I have a clear idea of the projects that I need to
complete as well as the interim
and final deadlines for each one.

■ ■ ■

339
I check out the credentials of the person who is
giving me advice since I value my own time.

■ ■ ■

340
I avoid equating the accumulation of tangible
wealth self-worth as I focus on my own definition
of success and achieving it for myself.

■ ■ ■

341
If I am thinking, "Where did the time go?"
I remind myself that I need to be working on
my time management skills and to become
more in control of how I spend my time.

■ ■ ■

342
I am constantly evolving.

■ ■ ■

343
I have all the time I need to get done
what is meaningful and crucial to me.

■ ■ ■

344
I am on time, every time, unless, on occasion,
I have a really good reason for being late.

■ ■ ■

345
I listen to my body so I can be in tune
with what my body needs.

■ ■ ■

346
I am powerful.

■ ■ ■

347
Today I am in control of each and every
minute of how I spend my time.

■ ■ ■

348
I make every second count.

■ ■ ■

349
Today is a new day and I have a positive attitude
about what is happening today.

■ ■ ■

350
Every day is a gift and I am
grateful for that gift of time.

■ ■ ■

351
Today I am making the time to appreciate all the
gifts I have been born with, and the ones
that I am cultivating through reading,
studying, observing, and listening.

■ ■ ■

352
I like myself.

■ ■ ■

353
My productivity soars when I work in collaboration.

■ ■ ■

354
"Time and tide wait for no man."
—Proverb

■ ■ ■

355
I am worthy of everything positive that
happens to me and I cause to occur.

■ ■ ■

356
Instead of letting procrastination waste and eat up
my time, I practice creative procrastination
whereby I substitute one priority task
for another priority task, accomplishing what
I want to do, and what I have to do, just
changing the order in which I achieve those goals.

■ ■ ■

357
I am making the most of every minute of time
that I am fortunate enough to be given.

■ ■ ■

358
The world may be unpredictable but I can
control the way that I react to whatever happens.

■ ■ ■

359
I am inspired by heroes and heroines.

■ ■ ■

360
I am inspiring.

■ ■ ■

361
I wake up energized and recharged,
excited about what today will hold,
living in the moment of today.

■ ■ ■

362
I take the time to enjoy looking at the photographs
or videos of family, friends, or work colleagues or
projects that I have taken or created.

■ ■ ■

363
I take the time to manage my time
without being too rigid or time conscious.

■ ■ ■

364
I gain strength as I work on what my legacy will be.

■ ■ ■

365
My time management skills are evolving
as my life and as business changes
and I embrace those advances.

■ ■ ■

Write your own time management affirmations

Use the space below to write down your own affirmations on time and time management:

1. _____

   _____.

2. _____

   _____.

3. _____

   _____.

4. _____

   _____.

5. _____

   _____.

PART II

TIME MANAGEMENT

Activities

Work-Related Activities

If this is a library book, to do these activities, especially the ones that require writing, take out a piece of paper and a pen or pencil, your journal, write on your computer, or even use your smart phone, if there is a way to use it for note taking.

If this is your own book, simply jot down your answers to the questions below. You might, however, want to make a photocopy of some of the activities before you enter your answers in case you want to redo these activities at different points in time to see if you have varied answers based on reading or rereading some or all of the affirmations in this book, additional readings, or workshops you attend.

1. Write down how long it currently takes you to find the following items or information in your office:

A pen _____

A calculator _____

The name and e-mail address of someone you are having lunch or dinner with for business over the next couple of weeks _____

_____

The population of your community _____

The date for your next performance review

_____

The registration information for an upcoming conference you are attending _____

_____

Look over your answers. Are there any supplies or piece of information that you need to develop faster access to? Yes _____ No _____

If yes, please list what those items are and what your target time is for finding those materials or information.

_____

_____

_____

2. Write down what you were told you were supposed to do for your current job on the very first day of the job. Think back and remember the job description and the related work activities you

were to be doing upon which you based your decision to take this job.

_____

_____

_____

_____

_____

Now write down a job description of your job as you have seen it evolve. What are the activities and tasks that you now realize are the key way you are being judged as effective in your job?

_____

_____

_____

_____

_____

Prioritize the tasks that your job requires of you. Write down what percentage of your day you spend on those priorities tasks. Is it 10%? 25% 50%? 100% zero time? _If the amount of time you are spending on the priority tasks of your job do not match the percentage of your day allotted to those tasks, make a commitment to change that (while you still have a job)._ If sales are your primary function, for example, what other tasks are you doing that are keeping you from doing sales? Can you delegate those other jobs to others?

Priority task(s) (ordered by importance)   Time spent

_____

_____

_____

_____

3. If you won ten million dollars tomorrow, what job would you want to have? Write your answer.

_____

If your current job is not your dream job, consider ways you can improve it:

_____

_____

_____

4. Keep a time log of one or two work days and evenings to track how you spend your time.

Work Time Log

Time   Activity

_____   Waking up

_____   _____

_____   _____

_____   _____

_____   _____

_____   _____

_____   _____

_____   _____

_____ _____

_____ _____

_____ _____

_____ _____

_____ Going to sleep

Review your log. Did you have a work (school) goal for the day? What was that goal?

_____

Did you accomplish that goal? If not, why not? Consider your work time log. Are there times during the day that you are more efficient?

5. Consider other jobs you have had.

_____

_____

Were you more or less productive than you are now?

___ more productive ___ less productive

___the same ___ other (fill in) _____

Write down the reasons for your answer.

_____

_____

_____

Is there any difference in you or in your work environment that might account for the difference in your productivity?

_____

_____

_____

What changes could you make in your work environment or how you go about your work that could aid your productivity?

_____

_____

6. Consider those you work with or for and their time management skills. If someone is especially productive, are there techniques or habits that you see him or her doing that you could emulate? If yes, what are those behaviors?

_____

_____

_____

7. Do you find that time "runs away" from you during your work day? Try using a timer — many smart phones have a timer function that you can set as needed and it will sound a bell or another kind of alarm— to help yourself to become more productive. If you spend too much time checking e-mails when you should be doing more concentrated work, try to limit the length of time you spend checking e-mails, as well as the frequency with which you do it.

8. If you are in school, or taking a course for job, career, or professional development, have you tried using the buddy system to be more accountable for what you are doing with your study time? Studying together and quizzing each other, especially if you are in the same classes, can be a productive way to study, particularly if you are at a similar level in class.

Some other school-related activities for improving your productivity include using a daily, monthly, or semester planner to set up when you will research, write, and rewrite term papers that are due as well as a study plan for upcoming tests so you are less likely to leave everything to the last minute.

Leisure-Related Activities

1. What are your favorite leisure time activities? Write down your top three:

    1. _____

    2. _____

    3. _____

2. When is the last time you did any of those activities?

    1. _____

    2. _____

    3. _____

Make a commitment to start enjoying your personal time more by making the time to do the activities you like to do. (If you are already taking the time to enjoy your preferred leisure time activities, consider if you want to change how often you achieve each one, or even how you go about it. For example, if you walk or go running alone but wish you had more leisure time to spend with friends or your romantic partner, perhaps you could start walking or running regularly with a friend or romantic companion?)

3. What is the most exciting and magical trip you can think of for you (or you and your romantic partner or family) to go on? How much will it cost? When could you get the time to do it? Discuss your ideas with your loved ones. Can you pick a date for this trip even if it is six months, a year, five years, or even longer in the future? Can you start putting money aside for this future trip? Use the space below to plan your trip.

_____

_____

_____

_____

_____

_____

4. If there are leisure time activities that you would like to do that you do not getting around to doing, fill out a time log for at least one leisure/weekend day so you see where you non-work time is actually being spent. Use the time log that follows, create your own on a blank piece of paper, or use your smart phone or computer to put the information. Begin with waking up, end with going to sleep, and chronicle, hour by hour, the activities that you participate in.

Leisure-Time Log

Time   Activity
_____   Waking up _____

_____

_____

_____

_____

_____

_____

_____

_____

_____

_____

_____   Going to Sleep

Review your completed log. Look for time that you might have spent differently—pursuing rewarding activities and spending time with those you care about—if you planned your day or structured your time differently. Consider any changes you might want to make to your leisure time so your non-work (or non-school) time is spent in a more satisfying way.

5. Describe what animal you see yourself as? A cat? A dog? An elephant? A horse? What is it about that

animal and how it seems to handle time that resonates with you?

_____

_____

_____

6. Make a list of your closest and best friends.

_____

_____

_____

Now write down when was the last time you spoke to each other on the phone, sent each other an e-mail or a text message, or especially got together in person? Try to figure out a plan that is workable so you can get together regularly with your friends if you have been too busy with work or other relationships.

7. Plan the ideal evening with your romantic partner. Where will you go? Will you cook dinner or go out to a restaurant? Will there be a band or guitarist playing music? What kind of food will you eat? Put as much time and effort into planning a night out with your loved one as you put into the work you do.

_____

_____

_____

_____

8 Clear up the clutter at home. If you need to start on another day besides today, pick a date and write it down:

_____

Now start by cleaning out your apartment or house, one closet, one room at a time. Clean out your garage and any other storage areas such as your attic or basement. Consider donating, recycling, or selling anything that you have not used in several years.

9. Do you wish you could read more in your leisure time? If yes, write down the top three books you plan to read and make a commitment to get to each one. Start by finding just one hour a day that you will devote to leisure reading. Don't have an hour a day? Try thirty minutes a day. It will quickly add up to 3-1/2 hours a week.

_____

_____

_____

_____

10. Think about your leisure time. If you have a traditional weekend off — from Friday after work till Sunday night—consider how many hours of leisure time that is available to you. Depending upon how many hours you sleep, you may have approximately 38 hours of non-work weekend

leisure time when you are awake. Out of those 38 hours, don't you owe it to yourself to take at least a couple of those hours to do something that you *really* want to do? Make a commitment to yourself that each weekend you will spend at least 2 to 4 hours making the most of your leisure time in non-chore or work-related ways that you enjoy. Block out fun leisure time for yourself — by yourself or with your loved ones—what I refer to in my book *Work Less, Do More* as "me" "us" or "we" time.

Use the space below to make leisure plans for an upcoming weekend:

Friday _____

Saturday _____

Sunday _____

PART III

THE THREE LESSONS MY FATHER

Taught Me on Time Management

My late father, William Barkas, DDS, who practiced dentistry for 40 years before he retired, provided me with three of my most powerful and enduring time management lessons. I pass those lessons on to you so you may instantly reap the benefits of these hard-won insights:

LESSON #1:
Get Out of the Mundane Day-to-day Routine and Make the Time to Be Together With Your Loved Ones Including Vacations

Being a dedicated and hardworking dentist, who worked on Saturdays and spent his one day off during the work week volunteering at a dental clinic, unfortunately left little time for family trips during my formative years. Yes, my father did take my sister and me bowling and ice skating at least once during the month on the weekends, and we went out to a movie and a fancy restaurant at least a twice a year to celebrate my mother or my father's birthday. But I cherished the longer leisure time together that is known as the family vacation, especially since my family had just three family vacations before I left home for college at the age of sixteen.

I know some of you may be thinking or even saying, "Kids will never feel you give them enough time." Not true! Kids, especially older children, teens, and adult children, have a need for family or extended family time that is "just right"—not too little and not too much so children or teens still have enough time available to them for their school or work commitments, friends, or other meaningful relationships.

The three trips that we went on as a family during my formative years loom so large in my memory bank that I do not think it is a coincidence that when my husband and I were living in Manhattan and house hunting, something inside me on a deep subliminal level called out for Connecticut, the location of the very first of those pivotal but infrequent family vacations when I was just three.

Yes, I am grateful that I gained a strong work ethic from my parents since so much of what I saw them doing when I was growing up was related to work, and preparing for work. That work ethic has certainly served me well in the demanding academic and professional careers I have pursued. But I learned from my father's extreme example of overemphasizing work and even being a workaholic (or addicted to working too much) that a balance of work and leisure benefits everyone.

I still struggle to control how much time I spend working and to have more fun in my life. When my children were little, if they had a half-day at school, I would plan an activity outside of the house for the afternoon. I did that because I knew that since I worked from home, I would be torn between wanting to continue working and paying attention to them. By going bowling, going to a local place where we could all paint our own pottery, out for lunch or for just an ice cream, I was trying to avoid passing on to the next generation the workaholism that had plagued my own formative years and my single ones. During their formative years, we also tried to go on a family vacation, whether it was a long weekend, a week, or ten days to two weeks, at least every other year. It is also my goal, now that our sons are grow up, as schedules permit, to be able to have family vacations again.

LESSON #2:
*Sometimes You Just Have to Stop Everything
and Find a Way to Be There
For Those You Care About*

It sounds like a cliché but the years galloped along and suddenly I turned around and I was in my forties, married, with two children of my own, and I found out that my 80-year-old beloved father was diagnosed with a brain tumor.

The next few months were a blur as I traveled back and forth at least once a week from my Connecticut home to the hospital on the Upper East Side of Manhattan where my father was being treated. He had successfully recovered from lung cancer seven years before so I tried to convince myself that despite the medical evidence to the contrary, he was going to get over this tumor and live at least a few more years.

But I was in denial. My father was getting much worse. Within two months, his health deteriorated at such a rapid rate that one day, seemingly without warning, he lost consciousness and ceased being the father that I had known, the one who had run a marathon in his sixties and who took long walks with my mother well into his late seventies. The chance to have conversations with my father—about his World War II experiences, about growing up during the Depression, about his dreams or fears—was gone in an instant.

That was the second dramatic time management lesson my father taught me—don't let day-to-day obligations keep you from a priority relationship or activity. Of course at the time there were reasons that seemed perfectly valid to explain why I could not spend any more time with my father at the hospital—childcare issues, work pressures, the time-consuming two hour commute each way from Connecticut to the hospital in uptown Manhattan. But once the finality of my father's situation became apparent, I realized that those reasons were pitiful excuses. I had let my day to day responsibilities and concerns prevent me from being there for my father even if it meant keeping a vigil at the hospital.

I emerged from that somber experience determined to have a renewed commitment to the people in my life.

I feel I've been trying harder to keep that commitment to my family and friends in the years since my father died. Just recently, I put aside a major project with a looming deadline to drive more than an hour away to have a reunion with an old friend that I had not seen for decades. There was a time when I would have cancelled because of my workload especially if I had a pressing deadline.

LESSON #3:
If You Fulfill Your Own Dreams,
You Will Be More Energized and Joyful,
And You Will Be a Role Model to Others

The third time management lesson my father taught me actually happened because of an epiphany two years after his death. My mother was trying to find something and she came upon a journal that my father had been keeping during his 64th year unbeknownst to anyone. He was documenting his thoughts during the year before his retirement.

My mother gave me the diary, my father's journal of his "countdown to retirement" year as he called his journal.

As I began reading his diary, I suddenly sobbed, overwhelmed with emotion as I learned, from my father's own words, that he had hoped to become a writer after he retired.

A writer! And I never knew that about my own father! But I could have helped him with his goal. I would have enjoyed being his mentor and then, when he finished his writing, reading his book. (I learned he had planned to write a nonfiction book about dealing with retirement.)

The sad reality—and this was the most powerful time management lesson my father taught me, albeit posthumously—was that he died, 15 years later, never having fulfilled his dream.

That was an even more powerful lesson than the first two—don't deny yourself the joy of fulfilling your dreams and goals. Fortunately, I've learned that lesson well and, just two years after my father's death, my lifelong dream of having a novel published was fulfilled when a mystery I co-authored with my husband Fred, *Untimely Death*, was published. (I might have had to found my own publishing company to publish it, but that did not matter; our novel was published and, as a bonus, it got excellent reviews and was even bought by a Swedish publisher and translated into Sweden; she brought us to Stockholm for an author tour of their edition.)

More recently, to make good on the dream we have both had for more than two decades of having one of our movies made, my husband Fred and I participated in something called The 48 Hour Film Project. We began at 7 p.m. on a Friday night and by Sunday night at 7, we had written from scratch, as well as filmed, edited (by the film editor on our team), and delivered to the competition a 4 minute film entitled "She Tweets." (Thanks to the cast, film editor, and musicians who helped us!) You can see our film at youtube.com. Whether it's four minutes, or four hours, the key point is that I did something to make my lifelong dream of having a movie made come true.

Do you have any dreams that you are putting off? One by one, find a way to begin fulfilling your dreams.

And even though my Dad did not fulfill his dream of becoming a "self employed author," as he put it in his diary, by keeping that diary, he at least was one step closer to fulfilling that dream since he was at least writing every day.

I hope someday to make that dream come true for him, by publishing his diary. In the meantime, I can reread his diary and enjoy sharing his thoughts, memories, and even remembering my father in a much more detailed way than I usually can, more than a decade after his death. For in the midst of his diary, I found a carbon copy of a letter that he wrote to me on February 24th, 1980.

The contents of the letter are special and uplifting, the encouragement you'd expect a father to extend to his grown daughter. But what stays with me as I stare at the carbon of that letter is what I learn about my father from that carbon copy. That he went to the trouble to make a copy of his letter to me, so he could put it in his journal, so he could remember his words to me, and commit those words to posterity. That's how important that letter to me was to him. He had to save a copy for himself. That says a lot to me about the man and about how he valued his communications with me.

Finally, I ask you to consider what lessons about time management your father or mother taught you? How have those lessons influenced how you approach each work day or your leisure time?

If you want to make changes in your approach to time, consider the lessons from your past; now take charge of reshaping how you handle your time in the present and future.

As my friend Mary, who is continuing to pursue her dream of directly plays, says, "Just keep on, keeping on."

I am making the most of each and every second, minute, hour, day, month, and year of my life because time is a gift and I appreciate the gift of time and of life.

Bibliography

Abraham, Jay. *Getting Everything You Can Out of All You've Got*. NY: St. Martin's Griffin, 2001.

Allen, David. *Getting Things Done*. NY: Penguin, 2002.

Blanke, Gail. *Throw Out Fifty Things*. NY: Hachette (Springboard Press), 2009.

Covey, Stephen. *7 Habits of Highly Effective People*. NY: Fireside Books, 1990.

Ferriss, Timothy. *The 4-Hour Work Week*. NY: Crown, 2007. (Expanded edition, 2010)

Frankl, Victor E. *Man's Search for Meaning*. NY: Touchstone Books, 1984.

Gilbert, Daniel. *Stumbling on Happiness*. NY: Vintage Press, 2007.

Hay, Louise. *I Can Do It: How to Use Affirmations to Change Your Life*. Carlsbad, CA: Hay House, 2004.

Lakein, Alan. *How to Get Control of Your Time and Your Life*. NY: New American Library, 1973.

LeBoeuf, Michael. *Working Smarter*. NY: Warner Books, 1982.

Luongo, Janet. *365 Daily Affirmations for Creativity*. Stamford, CT: Hannacroix Creek Books, Inc., 2005.

Mackenzie, Alec with Pat Nickerson. *The Time Trap*. 4th edition. NY: AMACOM, 2009.

Morgenstern, Julie. *Organizing from the Inside Out*. NY: Holt, 1998.

_____. *Time Management from the Inside Out*. NY: Holt, 2004.

Pausch, Randy and Jeffrey Zaslow. *The Last Lecture*. NY: Hyperion, 2008.

Rutherford, Robert D. *Just in Time*. NY: Wiley, 1981.

Yager, Jan. *365 Daily Affirmations for Creative Weight Management*. Stamford, CT: Hannacroix Creek Books, Inc., 2002.

_____. *365 Daily Affirmations for Happiness*. Stamford, CT: Hannacroix Creek Books, 2011.

_____. *Creative Time Management for the New Millennium*. Stamford, CT: Hannacroix Creek Books, Inc., 1999.

_____. *When Friendship Hurts*. NY: Simon & Schuster/Fireside Books, 2002.

_____. *Work Less, Do More: The 14-Day Productivity Makeover*. NY: Sterling Publishing, 2008.

Resources

www.drjanyager.com
My website with two free time management self-quizzes, reprinted from my book, *Creative Time management for the New Millennium*: "Could your time management skills use improvement" and "Do You need help delegating more effectively?" Includes a blog with entries on time management topics.

http://www.helpself.com/directory/time.htm
List of popular time management sites with a link to those sites.

http://www.greatmanagement.org
Selection of articles on time management.

www.selfgrowth.com
Free online resource with articles, videos, and newsletters related to the areas of success, love and relationships, health and fitness, money and careers, and lifestyle. Founded by David Riklan in 1998, it now has over 1 million visitors a month.

www.thelastlecture.com
Site devoted to Randy Pausch's last lecture as well as the book of the same name. Offers a link to watch "The Last Lecture" as well as an excerpt from the book of

the same name (*The Last Lecture*) and biographical information on the author and co-author.

http://blog.startupprofessionals.com/
Blog of Marty Zwilling, CEO and Founder of Startup Professionals, Inc., offering time management, leadership, and business advice for entrepreneurs and startup founders.

www.timeanddate.com
Free way to find out what time it is in any location around the world. Also offers calendars that you can print out and use for the current and future years.

National Association of Professional Organizers (NAPO)
www.napo.net
An association of professional organizers offering help with time management and cleaning up clutter, at home and in the office.

http://www.davidco.com/
Website of David Allen, bestselling author of *Getting Things Done* and time management speaker. Offers free articles for downloading.

http://www.juliemorgenstern.com/blog/
Blog of time management author and speaker Julie Morgenstern (*Organizing from the Inside Out*).

http://www.fourhourworkweek.com/blog/
Blog by Tim Ferriss, author of *The 4-Hour Work Week*.

Index

About the Author

Jan Yager, Ph.D., president of Timemasters.com, is a productivity coach and author; she has also being offering workshops and giving speeches on time management based on her original research for more than two decades.

Dr. Yager is the author of 30 books translated into 24 languages in the areas of business, relationships, and other topics including three other books on time management: *Creative Time Management for the New Millennium; Work Less, Do More;* and *Creative Time Management.* Other business books include *Business Protocol; Grow Global; Effective Business & Nonfiction Writing;* and *Productive Relationships.*

To book this author/time management expert for your next meeting, contact your favorite speakers bureau or send an e-mail directly to the author at yagerinquiries2@aol.com. (To see clips of Jan Yager being interviewed on major TV shows as well as speaking on time management, go to www.youtube .com and put "Jan Yager" in the search engine.) For more information on Jan's coaching, speaking, or writings, visit the author's website: www.timemasters .com.

Other Affirmation Books
Published by Hannacroix Creek Books, Inc.
www.hannacroixcreekbooks.com
(Available at your favorite online or local bookstore)

365 DAILY AFFIRMATIONS FOR CREATIVITY by Janet Luongo
Foreword by Jack Canfield (co-author, *Chicken Soul for the Soul* series)
Affirmations to inspire creativity, divided into 12 categories with an additional 60 exercises for individuals and managers.
"Janet Luongo will take you on a journey of self-discovery and self-awareness tht will lead you to a whole new level of creativity."
—Janet E. Lapp, RN, Ph.D., author, *Positive Spin*

365 DAILY AFFIRMATIONS FOR HAPPINESS by Jan Yager, Ph.D.
Upbeat and inspiring, this book about happiness has an introduction, affirmations, exercises for work and for personal time, a bibliography, and resources.
"Dr Jan Yager has done a terrific job with her book which will help guide YOU to happiness. I used affirmations at Zappos and use them in my new company because they work! Great job Dr. Jan Yager! —Dr Vik, former trainer at Zappos shoes

365 DAILY AFFIRMATIONS FOR CREATIVE WEIGHT MANAGEMENT y Jan Yager, Ph.D.
These affirmations reinforce a positive attitude toward a readers' body image and physical self, whatever their weight, including suggestions about what to do besides grabbing food out of boredom and other emotions, or just plain habit.
"Provides inspiring, practical guidance for developing healthy attitudes regarding health and weight management."—Jeffrey R. Wilbert, Ph.D., co-author, *Fattitudes*®

365 DAILY AFFIRMATIONS FOR FRIENDSHIP by Jan Yager, Ph.D.
(Due out soon)
Includes introduction about friendship by this friendship coach and author of *Friendshifts* and *When Friendship Hurts* plus activities for enhancing friendship at work and in your personal life.

Breinigsville, PA USA
18 February 2011
255784BV00004B/1/P